Winner of the 2005 Carolina Wren Press Poetry Contest

"When Robert Graves wrote 'Nothing promised that is not performed' he was in the thrall of the *White Goddess*. This poet, whose goddess/ muse is an intriguingly contemporary Persephone, composes and performs such works as 'The Gift,' 'Hades,' 'After *Hysterics*,' and the title poem with the luxurious patience only a marvelously ripened spirit can achieve; that attentive languor and the spell of authenticity it begins instantly to cast, manage to be intoxicating and sobering in the same draught. An impassioned elixir, deeply alluring, strongly recommended. And, yes, here in *Suddenly, Fruit* all promises are kept."

—**WILLIAM PITT ROOT**, 2005 CONTEST JUDGE

Suddenly, Fruit

Linda Tomol Pennisi

Poetry Series #9

CAROLINA WREN PRESS
Durham, North Carolina

The mission of Carolina Wren Press is to seek out, nurture, and promote literary work by new and underrepresented writers, including women and writers of color.

Editor: Andrea Selch

Design: Lesley Landis Designs
Cover Image: "Pomegranate Orb" © 2006 Sue Sneddon
Author Photograph: Joanne Caslake

This publication was made possible in part by generous grants from the North Carolina Arts Council. In addition, we gratefully acknowledge the ongoing support made possible through gifts to the Durham Arts Council's United Arts Fund.

Library of Congress Cataloguing-in-Publication Data

Pennisi, Linda Tomol, 1952-
Suddenly, fruit / Linda Tomol Pennisi.
p. cm.
ISBN 0-932112-52-8
I. Title.

PS3616.E56S83 2006
811'.6--dc22

2006016563

Suddenly, Fruit

FOR JOHN, ANNIE AND JOHN

Contents

ONE

I can hear, underground, that sucking and sobbing,
In my veins, in my bones I feel it—
The small waters seeping upward,
The tight grains parting at last.

—Theodore Roethke

Cooking

Off the coast of New Zealand, a giant
squid caught today, and I'm wondering
what this NPR feature has to do
with me, because the story
tugs and roils while I slice carrots
and chop onions and the soup
peaks to a sudden boil. Turning
the heat to medium-lo, I wish
I had listened more carefully.
It was the first time a squid that size
had been caught alive, the woman
was saying, when the phone rang,
or the doorbell, or one of the kids
needed me for a clean pair of sweats.
I've been thinking about having my body
cut open. It's not that I'm diseased,
but lumps are appearing near the surface,
and it's the first time I'm seeing
loss in terms of addition—real, touchable
newnesses, like the one just beside
my navel. The other night I dreamt
it was growing, roping
bulbously around my back, cutting off
something vital. That I loved giving birth
makes it ironic, I guess—an out-of-control
umbilical cord, the thing to finally
do me in. I don't mean to suggest
that the squid is linked in some
mythic way to my birth or death,
or that the soup or the kids or the vegetables
are in any way connected. It's just
that sometimes a dream emerges,
and a segment from *All Things Considered*
slips into my kitchen, and then the kids
drift in, and I've got this knife
in my hands, and I'm cooking.

Pageants

I keep searching for religion, but the closest
I come is O'Keeffe's lilies, or my dwarf
half-cousin, Mary, stepping from death into the porch light's
yellow semi-circle in a dream,

Don't be afraid. I'll stay with you, she says.
For a while, I'm comforted. But when my throat
closes off and I try to cry, *Mary!*
the name gets stuck, weighted

with pageants and powder blue shawls,
and the rubber doll I pretended was Jesus,
swaddling it in last year's musty blanket
near where my breasts hadn't begun to bloom.

Chosen to play Mary, my daughter, six then,
broke down on her way up the aisle.
The cardboard donkey she held like a skirt
around her, clumsy. A throng of angels

awaiting their cue. In the vestibule
she clung to my legs before leaving
for Bethlehem; the donkey slid to the floor
as she tried to escape it. You can do it,

I urged her into a sanctuary of expectant
faces. The congregation smiled, laughed
even, as she silently wept on her way toward the town.
It was too much for her. Every day for a month

when she went off to school, she cried,
as if every journey was that difficult journey,
that half-smiling donkey still on her hips, and she losing
control of where it might take her.

Behind My Tongue

Fifteen years ago,
the word *daughter* formed in my mouth
and I birthed it.
Two years before, I mouthed
the word *son.*

Words spring
from chambers of my body:
tear
red
tunnel
home.

I dress my rooms
in words: grocery lists
magnetized to the refrigerator,
letters floating in bowls
of milk or broth.
The ouija moves my fingers
to the muse: bloom.

At home, the iris ruffles
its edge,
stem reaching earthward,
the green of my eye
hunting
the lush word inside.

Sunday Afternoons

In her red wool coat, Persephone
is hiding in the circle of spruce trees
around the corner of the house.
She does not want to go in,
does not want to close her eyes
or her nose, or especially
her mouth.

They will let me up again,
she reminds herself.
In a little while,
they will let her up.

Persephone always cries when they find her
and lead her to the blue bed.
When they hold her down,
she kicks and writhes.

She cries out when they come at her
with the tube. When they fill her with soap
and water, she swallows her screams.
Her little sister told her,
once, to be still

and think of flowers.
Inside her eyes, red roses.
Or peonies.

Persephone Meets Christ

Funny, how she thought he
could save her. It was one of those
warm spring days, the kind where the buds
are full as bees, and ready.
It had been a hell of a winter,
and she was just coming out of it.
She spotted him on the corner,
with a crowd around him.
They looked at him as if
he were some kind of god,
and she could see why.
He had the kindest eyes and a soft voice
that made her want to listen.
Oh, and a ponytail down to his ass.

Soon they were having coffee
and she was telling him all about the guy
who kept bringing her down.
No matter how she tried, she couldn't
get away for good. When she wasn't living
with this guy, she'd go dancing with her girlfriends
or just hang out at her mother's house,
altogether happy. But then, sure enough,
by the time the apples would fall in October,
she'd go out, find herself
heading down to see him, miserable.

This god-guy was sympathetic and wished
he could help, but he had his own problems.
A father who had some kind of hold on him
and wanted him back home.

Sure, some jealous guys around town
were giving him a hard time, so in a way
he was ready to leave, but home
was a long way off and the trip
would be a rough one. He said he'd be back;
that he'd come every spring
if she would. She walked him as far
as the field. They didn't bother to kiss.

A Body in the Pond
May 3, 1909

She should be
In the kitchen,
Filling the chipped enamel basin
For his bath,
Mixing flour and milk
In a china bowl.
Sometimes he finds her

Across the hall, rocking
On the sun-bleached floor,
Or sleeping stiffly, legs
Straight down, arms extended
Over the angel wing quilt,
Stitched together years ago,
When she carried babies
And lost them.

Starched doilies over thin
Tattered chair arms in the parlor.
The settee covered with a sheet,
A wedding gift of velvet,
Barely touched.
Piano keys, under the dusty wooden lid,
Soundless.

In the kitchen
The screen swings
As if she'll step back in.
Before he looks,
He imagines her
Squatting in the chicken coop,
Cotton gown hiked high
Above her knees,
Hands rummaging straw.

Collecting small white eggs,
Fast as she can,
For his breakfast.

In a Room at the Tate
The Lady of Shallot

The woman has readied the boat.
Beneath the willow, she lowers herself into it.
The whole kingdom will hear singing.   She has brought
Christ along for the ride.   In a room at the Tate,
a boy sketches her hair in the last yellow
edge of light.   He is right to pull back.
This Lady.   This painting.   This
cool room.   Tourists.   I slip inside her woods
to insist,   *There is no spell. THERE IS
NO SPELL.*   She had grown used to mirrors, to the hands
that were hers translating the living into cloth,
to the self between her image and the seen, her eyes the axis,
the real just over her shoulder, coming through her

to the glass, through her to the loom. Desire
(his brow his hair his voice) cracked the face between them;
desire (in its wine-colored cloak) walked her here,
to this boat shaped like a sad smile.   Now, so long, so
many long years after, a boy is coming   close

his breath on her face, straight on it.
He could get stuck in his seeing,   her looking back,
the way her pale hand still holds the chain.
He could make it too
important, the long white sleeve spilling

over the water. Could he
slip into it: the boat, her half-parted lips, the first notes
of her death-song? From firm ground,
I mouth a warning.   But he is studying the slope of her
belly, the shadow between shoulder and chin,

a space there,   just near her hair, a darkness,
a yearning.   And the sound I attempted is rounding
the woods, the water, the room
at the Tate, returning now to the mouth
of this woman, a casual
tourist. A hum, which moves.

Flower-Writing

I'll paint what I see—
what the flower is to me.
             —Georgia O'Keeffe

One hundred woman-flowers bloom
A ruffle-edged garden. She weaves
Perennials on canvas: a life-loom
Of morning glory with black, eve

Of the day lily. A rose reclines,
Loose bud of pinkness, one lip
Curved, on the verge of open. Entwined
With herself, the sweet pea slips

From white to pink to plum. Canna
Buds, blossoms, bleeds, becomes
Demeter and Persephone both: a hand
That won't go under. Her flowers succumb

To nothing. The petunia refuses to die.
Clothed in purple, its power
Unfurls before us; defies
The coming cold, the darkening hour.

The Front Row

Each Sunday, behind
a drape the color of wine
they sit, only shoulders and faces
visible to the congregation.
Eyes on the preacher,
the sopranos pass time
passing their hands along
each others' hands and forearms,
barely touching,
a drizzle of fingertips
calling sensation up
to the surface like new grass.
Their way to get through it—the long
unraveling of rights and wrongs,
Christ doing this and doing that.
They perk up, sometimes,
with word of Eve's birth pains
or one of the Marys, quivery
when he talks of the serpent
or angel. In the feel
of another girl's flesh,
they are learning themselves.
They take turns,
five minutes touching, five
being touched.

In Castle Rest

Flat on his back now, Theo recalls
the small cot in the Greek village,
where he lay on the edge

of sleep as a boy, willing himself
not to move. His mother, wise woman,

knowing the value of flesh,
would place a spoonful of silkworm eggs
in the hollow of his chest.
When they start to move,

she'd whisper, *call me.*
All day I see this old man
as an obedient boy. I wash his blue stillness,

the cup his chest makes with each

movement of air.
Was there sound to the hatching?
40,000 little bursts of song—

the finale of an almost inaudible
display of fireworks,

a series of pops endlessly strung,

then tapering? After,

was there one movement,
an egg-shaped sea,
rippling? Or had he trained

himself, his alert flesh, to separate
one barely visible body
from the next, the way one can feel
sand, or rain?

When he called, his mother
would come for the trembling
mass and spoon it back to her own breasts
so he could sleep.

Could Theo ever truly sleep
those nights, his flesh part of something

else now? When he tried,
was it there, dream-silk,

extra threads of nerve
weaving figure-eights behind his eyes?

Awake most nights in Castle Rest,
Theo must be waiting for the time

to call out; for her to come.
Perhaps, still, in his deep eyes
dance cream-silk

wedding gowns, kimonos untying
at the waist, layers of slips beneath dresses,
silk beneath them, touching

the silk lips they cover.

Planting, Memorial Days

Up the steep cemetery hill, the girls
work small legs as if on the verge

of fairy tale or magic, or some myth about flowers
or wells, the watering can swinging between,

Christ looming that way in white
marble over their small heads,

his own head bowed and crowned,
the cross jutting densely into cloudlessness

on a day not so unusual, really, their ragged overalls
dragging a little, Mother and the geraniums

wilting against the stones above. It is a vision I return to,
this time of day, when the sun hits my neighbor's

roof urgently in its setting, as if touching
the shoulder of someone before parting, remembering

something that needs saying this time,
Wait a minute, just one more moment,

please. There is a voice I'm trying to find
to help me say this, whatever it is, to you now,

one which needs to be drawn from the mouth
of the smallest girl, but hers is closed so resolutely

in her trudging, I can see her neck muscles
bulge, a song trying to bloom before

it dies. Maybe Christ hanging there,
His quiet beads of marble blood, or the way

Mother brings their deaths to life—
Father's mother, three small brothers,

two sisters—while she scoops earth
from itself, making room.   At the top of the hill

the way Mother makes their hot deaths bloom—
typhoid, diphtheria, little Carmen

shoved into a neighbor's scalding kettle,
where spice and juices overlap

his scream—makes the small girl's song
unworthy, not worth releasing.

Her grandmother, absent for a daughter's
sudden death and burial, split

the earth so she could know her child
was dead. Two nights ago in a dream

I turned my head so a tube
inserted through my mouth could find its way

to my heart. Drawing back
on a syringe, a woman resembling me

aspirated parts of a girl from between beats.
A microscope, a sudden protrusion

at the room's center, gleamed. My own
breath there on the lens, fogging it.

Missing

From the kitchen window, Persephone
keeps her eye on the field,
where it curves against the woods;
arranges spring flowers
in a bowl, tulips and irises.
She waits all day.
At night, she prays and waits.

Her girl is twelve now,
going into the seventh grade.
In the brush beneath the tall maples,
her pink and white bike
was found three weeks ago,
papers scattered like flags,
crayola markers strewn nearby, a small
chaos of washable color.
Persephone, cutting thick stems on a flat
board, knows there are holes in the earth.
She knows.

A minister's wife, she has been
busy seeing the good, so much of her
time spent looking skyward,
noting the way the sun
spreads to all. She mentioned
the holes. But how she wishes
she had marked them. Persephone
would like to mark God,
but she can't let herself
think it. *Here,*

she should have said, and
Here. An X near the sweet-smelling roses.
One through both hands
of the clock at noon. A black X
on the road from church
where her girl was
last seen.

Instrumentals

How many times have I used the word *mouth*?
And *flower* and *bloom,* and last year
red sang everywhere like a young friend

who keeps calling for advice on love
or the (im)possibility of casual sex. Once this guy
read aloud to her as they hiked
in the Berkshires. They even danced
in the Berkshires to no music. Last week,
she ushered for a theater group,
a funky little Boston troupe with blue heads

and faces, while I half-hid my eyes
at the foot of a hospital bed, learning Death's
personification. If I were casting,
I'd have thought that empty-mouthed,
white-eyed creature too clichéd.
Hyperbolic. I mostly listen to instrumentals

these days. I'm developing an aversion
to characterization and point
of view. This morning the wordless cello
says more than I could ever hope to,
and in *Another Silent Night,* is it the piano's
high-octaved rambling that pulls
the painful flutes toward home?

Once we stopped in Linguaglossa—
a village part way up
Mt. Etna. Don't be fooled by the beauty
of that word—*Linguaglossa.*
You might think you can hold
its fluid in your mouth
forever. You might be sucked
into seeing the tongue
as power.

TWO

Glass

Arms to the elbow
in soapy water   I search
for the last goblet   a curve
of laughter from the night
before   a dream so clear
I can see through it
My thoughts caress
its slipperiness   the concave
hollow place within
the long stem that makes the flower
a possibility   I handle it
gently
knowing how fragile
these things can be
a warm breath on cold glass
my reflection
in the kitchen window

The Gift

It's not what I asked for, really,
curving over my navel in the mud room this way
like a child picking lint in the bath.
Bending over myself in green-walled
darkness is not what I asked for, but dreams can't be
ordered, no 800 number, no request line
to fit this day's mood to the image of my choice.
My dream-fingers loosen a sticky string,
something mucoid and horribly lovely
till it slopes and opens to the coin of daylight
where my genitals hide. The doorbell's shrill ring,
the dog's sharp bark are not
what I asked for, the dream intruding upon itself
like a prolapsed cord, or a billowy curtain suddenly
sucked against the screen,
just when you thought from your place
on the inside that you'd see something
that could change your life. But the wind
kicks up, that's something to count on,
and in the right now of this dream
I don't want to make coffee for three stiffly
dressed strangers, or pull heavy white cups
from the shelf. If I say, *How warm*
for this time in October! or *Sugar?*
And cream? the emptiness will vanish,
the need to fill it, the way my body curves
to hold it, my mouth a place for reverberation,
my flesh a chute, the voice a child in a playground
pushing off till the mouth
emits an *oh,* an *ah,* a hard *k.*

* * *

On a high rock is Grasmere,
the curving voice takes the hills,

the lakes, the bodies of sheep. Can you hear
it rest its red hands on the restless lake?
The bell of it rising just after it dies like so many little Christs?
The flowers retrieve it, white bodies
 gathering, a net now toward the east, now west.
My atheist aunt's voice rises from a coffee can,
A&P, Red Circle, Extra Fine. I save her death
in the aroma, the fine grains. I bury our infidelity—
the priest we sat at her bedside, reading
his thick psalms as she eyed us from behind
the smell of urine and morphine drapes. Deeper in the grains,
her laugh, the way it penetrated our house when she'd visit,
filled chipped soup bowls and found even the cat
covering its mess deep in the bin. After many years of it,
she did not believe in marriage. She did not believe
in democracy or the afterlife of the soul.
Put her hands in the sandy soil, though,
her oversized Hungarian hands, and she would attest to
the earth's willingness to take what is placed inside
and issue change, the miracle of the New Jersey tomato.

* * *

Change is not what I asked for. The grandmother
I knew only from photos against a Pennsylvania
backdrop of coal and loss, eyes me now
from Hungary, 1908, from an oval-framed
studio of cream roses and lace.
Outside the photo's translucent window, the Danube
stirs and heaves, I know it. Hillsides mouth
a foreign language in red-peppered words
I understand. Today
her voice takes on other
voices. 1956. The square littered
with Russian tanks. The women of Budapest

erupting from houses, glass jars
held before them like shields.
The gift of a jar filled with fruit,
how fruit can be used as a defensive weapon,
the fingers dipping into the cooked and sugared plum,
emerging dark and sweet enough, enticing,
fingers smearing last year's plum jam
on peepholes, covering each tank's eye
with jam made from three trees along the back
fence. You do what you have to, you do what makes the enemy
rise high so his fall is final, and sometimes you hide your face
when his head emerges, sometimes you watch him
poke up to see where he's going, the bullet
from the sharpshooter's gun going clean into his eye,
his neck, his right cheek.

*   *   *

In a dream it's time for me to tango
with the professor of philosophy across the white
marble floor. Amazed, I let my three inch heels
take me, a filmy gown
the shape tonight I'm meant to fill.
There is a gloriousness to this dance,
this body, the way it takes the dips, the bends,
the way it is
the dance—such torrents, such
blank unswerving whiteness
where pouring now like milk
from an overflowing cup, pouring now
from its edges, the room—these
dancing women. We
have work to do; there is blood
on the white marble floor.

* * *

You do what you have
to, you take what feeds you and make it
work. The well inside, empty, needs you to place
your lips now to your own ear and breathe
the words *shh, shimmer, hum.* The fruit,
the washed plum heavy as time
in your hand, full as the new moon, as your own womb
spilling with power, saying, *Ah, you didn't know,*
did you, the power of the cooked, the sugared,
the veins running far beneath the skin,
how they shapechange, colorchange,
clarify, obscure? The gift of the one there with bent fingers
stirring the pot, pronouncing time now
for this; time for that.

Hades

It happens all the time: the older man
wants a girl. He has to hand it
to his god-brother, it's the perfect solution,
really, giving in to Demeter's wailing,
her threats to starve everyone if she doesn't get her way.
All he has to do is slip a few seeds
between the girl's lips and she'll keep coming
back for more. At first he was pissed:
Who the fuck does Demeter think she is, just because
she's alone and bored, a withery old bitch,
Zeus lets her have her way like this?
Probably wishes she'd been the one in the field
swallowed by his flowery cock.
But this part-time arrangement,
the more he thinks about it, is the best kind.
Six months on, six off; he's horny nearly all the time
just knowing he won't get sick of her.
He never needs to see her fat and pregnant,
and the kids, of course, will prefer to stay with Grandma.
When Persephone returns, she'll be freshly tanned—
thankful for the time away.
This is the way the gods planned it, working
always for their own good.

What We See Simply as Light

Nightly, the fireflies
pulse their call for sex
into the tall and swaying lupines,
the bushy roses. How orderly
the two thousand species
mark themselves, avoiding those
whose rhythms do not fit
their own patterns of light
and dark, the intervals
between. The impulse too
protects them from predators, the flash
a sign of bitterness.
Yet the call, male to female,
not a foolproof foil for death:
See the frog beneath the mint leaves
who has eaten so much
hunger, he glows.

How They Find Angels

Today Blake is there,
the garden thick with color,
and Mrs. Blake, sitting cross-legged
beneath a peach tree, the poet
reclining near a weeping
plum. She reads *Paradise Lost*
aloud, while he listens,
then she spreads
the wings between her legs,
showing him, again, where they
come from, men like him.

He's all for it—the impractical
doors of garments gone,
her pulling his eyes close,
the dark opening
where God is.
She remembers men
like Donne—revealers
of their women's mystic
books. Now in the noontime sun
she shows him the first gray hairs—
how he must enter them.

After Hysterics

After the theater, stepping into new snow, I pull on
my mask with my scarf and gloves. The actress had forced me,
singing a song in Swahili I had never heard,
but somehow knew, as if her soul were flowing from her
open mouth. She'd taken us through the days
before surgery—sitting on an imaginary toilet, dipping
her hand as if into a well, dribbling the last of her red self
onto parchment she would bury, then dipping
again, more deliberately, bringing her last menstrual blood
to her face. Walking toward the café, my husband imagines
our friend, Jim's, reaction—*I don't mind menstruation,
it's the glorification*
of menstruation I object to. We laugh through sambuca
and coffee, peach crumb pie, keep our conversation light
as the flakes swirling outside the green-framed window.
We avoid talking about the play, the actress who played all
parts: self, husband, the African nurse
who had raised her to sing, to bury her hair
and nails, to see her body as power.
When she comes in and sits a table away, her face unstreaked
and smiling, I have to keep my mask from slipping, from revealing
my own cheeks, stained now with blood
and salt. Like the surgeon who took her womb, her song
in the dark theater laid me open. All I have left
is seeping out—a mouth slowly going silent.
The mask is talking, planning the menu for Saturday night, words
like "lamb" and "veal." I am two people, and the one
who is speaking has nothing to say.

Feeding, 5:00 p.m.

This evening, where the brush begins,
the deer are licking Lot's wife. Their long silent tongues

groove her imposed smoothness, the unforgiving
hardness where her flesh had been. It is almost painful

and they know it, their slow flesh taking slow laps, sculpting,
shaping her into something more resembling a woman.

Their touch unlike any she remembers, she surrenders.
From so much motionlessness she had craved

transcendence. Now the soul's release into fleshy mouths,
its long slide down sloping throats, the bellies'

still-decipherable shapes, earth-smells—
twigs and grasses, juniper berries.

In the Next Field

This Thanksgiving, my mother wears a green sweater; her eyes
somewhere between moss and the sea.
Leaving the house for my third walk,
I let myself notice an almost imperceptible
tremble to her head, the Katherine Hepburn type,
as if she's beginning an incessant yes to something.
Usually hatless, she covers her bald spot with a knit
beret, a new thing. At home one night I dreamt this field
I now walk by, how the air was dark and sweet,
overripe with apples. In that dream a young man
calmed me, seeing the explosion in the next
field as a display of fireworks. I could see then sparks
arranging themselves for a slow, choreographed
descent. I must ask what he knows
of bridges. I am crossing one now and it used to sing.
As a girl, I would stand on the porch and listen
for its hum—my parents' return. Nine days ago,
my daughter's picture was buried with her other grandfather.
Her heart-shaped face, tanned and pensive, has been closed there
all week, and is closed there still.
I'm trying not to think of the darkness. If only I could see
sparks. If I could hear, in the distance, a humming.

* * *

In one week's time, she perfected the Bach
piece, witnessed death, and decided there must

be a God. I bought her a red pepper
to ease the pain. The market carried pomegranates
that week, but it was the pepper

I'd stuff in her stocking when she was small.
It was how she knew there was a Santa Claus,
because there hadn't been

31

a pepper—her favorite food—in the fridge.
Now she explains there is

a higher power, for Papa did not keep
his eyes rolled back nor his mouth
ghoulishly open. Just before he died,

he killed Death, she writes in a poem.
Then his eyes came back; his mouth
became his mouth again.

* * *

My husband had prepared
the room. The children's pictures
near the hospital bed. An easy chair.
A color t.v. The king sized bed on the far
white wall, a ledge for his mother's
blossoming grief. Outside the double window,
the feeder, moved from the living-
room's view, provided color, a little—
magic? I had never seen life
ushered out so beautifully before.
And after, the room re-positioned, restored
to its former grace. From the outside, you
might never know what took
place there. You would need to put your weight
behind the dresser. A dime-sized hole
at the baseboard held a clear
plastic tube. Discreetly, it had carried
oxygen from the next
room. The noisy machine
which produced it, like a wild,
unnameable creature, hissed
and popped and spattered.

* * *

The air today sharp with manure
and gunshots, and the weasel my father finally trapped

hangs, delicate and shadowy, from the stable's
front corner, closest to the road. Since he was a boy,

my father has always loved pigeons,
how they ascend from the shit-
filled coop, yet always return.
Lately, the weasel has been dragging

their soft round bodies, one by one,
into an opening in the ground that seems

impossibly small. It held the final
pigeon in its teeth when the trap,

like God's fingers, snapped.
Almost eighty now, my father

swears off pigeons. The weasel,
still alive when he found it,

was eating and suffering, festering
with rage. With his .22,

he had to finish it off.
Now when he looks up

what catches his eye
is the weasel's dark dangling.

Its pointed mouth at eye level, still
a little red, but quiet.

* * *

What does the word carnival
have to do with any of this?
My father-in-law looked up
at the moment he died.

Last summer at the ballpark, a sign
on the ticket booth:
Property of Holy Angels
Carnival.
In a world of hot dogs
and cherry slushes, an invitation
into fleshlessness
and tumbling, a little sleight

of wing, an air parade.

I think of flight.
In a burst of early snow,
cardinals,
like clots, dislodge
from the sky.

Such maddening
hunger. The feeder
oozes. And sings.

* * *

For weeks before his death,
he dreamed he arrived, empty-
pocketed, at the market.
Today at Hall's
Big M, a bin of exotic fruit

imported for the holiday:
star-fruit, papayas, pomegranates.

My purse bulges with coins
and twenties.

I want to smear my face with the seeds
of pomegranates. I want
my hair sticky-sweet with papaya;
in my mouth—

I can taste it—
the sky.

Persephone at Gethsemane

Among the lilies and the olive trees,
he looked for me.
He cried *Father,* it's true,
but all the while his face
was buried deep in the hyacinth's
blue glow, and he was breathing
air the flowers had already let go of.
I knew what was coming—the tea-colored
wounds, the incessant end.
Here the apricot—
a yolk inside a velvet shell—already
a little bruised. He wondered how
I keep doing it—the up, the down,
the blooming, the dying.
Among petals and shoots
still bearing the scent
of another world,
he grew calm here,
calling the father who wouldn't answer.

The Hotel Gardens

And then, you see, it's the moment just before
the undoing, the fountain still rising, the sibilance of its rising
like some childhood girlfriends wanting your attention

or Mother saying *Shhhhh* so loudly you could laugh
(A man in plum watches you listen) or just
                                        break down

and weep. And now, you see, it's the coming apart,

(he leans over the pool, tossing) not the physics of falling not the
gravity
but the splitting first, you see, water
separating for an instant in the air, the plosives, the bursting,

this hanging apart for an instant in the 3 p.m. light, like the *p*
in the word *splash* having its moment
alone, this brief
unintruded upon shape, this flute note, this out-into-the-world
move that makes a droplet

a droplet,

which thrills you here on this stone bench and makes your heart
(a flock of ducks)
bound a little with possibility, your skirt flower

asymmetrically near a bed of pink zinnias, gold mums.

The Fig Tree

And so the woman, each year, dug a trench to bury her tree.
It reminded her of home—the sun-drenched soil
near Linguaglossa and the kind of sweetness

that perishes fast. She taught herself how to keep alive

in frigid Syracuse what should thrive only in hot,
dry weather. And all the while

twelve children grew. Each year as she pressed
and eased, the tree bent its thin trunk,
and kept promising beneath

January's white suffocation.
In her silent bed
the woman imagined she was the tree

lying cold there and still.

How she loved the shovel's first scrape,
its rhythmic journey toward her. Arms

that would reach into earth-smells

and dusk. And sometimes she became
the one unearthing

the fig, and she even felt what that one might

if the tree never revived. It was the way she passed
her nights and winters, imagining

the sweetness, imagining herself
the tree.

Orpheus

Nearby, women wash their hair
in the river. The current
lifting and fanning, their long hair
billowing as if wind were the movement
beneath. And the fish silvering deep,
flashing. Then his song intrudes
sweetly at first like a soft-blown
breath near the ear, or like sun-shadows

in the oak above. So they track it—
not a hunt or a chase but a discovery,
like parting the reeds to find
a child at the mouth of a cry.
Then the god's beautiful need, the form of it,

attaching to the song so the song
becomes more than sound. As the partially nude
boy who tips the vase becomes
the fountain, so Orpheus is
the longing he shapes and pours
into the forest incessantly.
Look, they say, *Look you can't keep*

this up we will be a place
for you. But the mourning doves
loop his hymn and a pierced
doe bleeds into it and a red squirrel
runs its trills in wide circles.
And so many women come.
Stones, smooth and egg-shaped,
click alive in their palms, trembling

with music. And the song grows
too sweet, begins to damage skin
because it has a body now that won't touch them,

hurts their mouths
when they see its full pink tongue,
and their erratic hearts grow loud
inside their breasts, while Orpheus
keeps pulsing his song into everything.

Form

Persephone is on stage in the small dark
coffee house, and she is blooming.
Standing in one beam of light,
she is not the poppy or the rose
or the tulip, unfolding
a slow bud of red or deep plum,
though she reads of blood
and death. Tonight
Persephone is the forsythia.
She comes in yellow bursts
from tongue-tip and fingertip;
a million pores zing open
to birth a star-blossom each.
Arranging her limbs in the pendulous
air, Persephone becomes
the poem's body—
a golden bush
against the dark.

The Gap

The traffic on the highway, always coming
and going. Listen with your eyes
open. Close the shades, keep out
the light sweeping across the dresser—
the bisque statue of mother and children,
her one arm broken at the shoulder, a picture hat
from a friend's wedding, mint
green and flaccid. I used to lie
for hours in that searchlight of sound,

that swoosh, that wave, the child's bounce
from the trampoline above her friends' upturned
faces, peaking, returning, her long brown hair
hitting her shoulders a millisecond
later. Sometimes I stayed up at night
crescendoeing, or wanting to, and when the traffic
grew light after one or two, when the sound
almost stopped, I was terrified,
trapped in a shrieking silence,
magenta or flashing red.

When I talk about that silence, I can't
get it across the way I would like. We might be caught
in a braid of conversation, words overlapping
so fast we can't see the in-between, the gap, the place
where words aren't, where deer
come out at night in search of berries
near that small dark road
between mountains, or the space in the yard
that would be empty if not for the birch tree's
ruminations. We could be talking,
talking, the air in the restaurant full of verbs

and rattling dishes, the smell of shrimp,
bananas sizzling on a portable cart.
And don't ask me why
but I am still the girl at the apex
of her jump, then I'm coming down
but there's no trampoline, no surface

to return to, my friend's face slipping by me
like memory, and I try to grab onto it
the way the guy falling in the movies
catches onto a ledge, and hangs there
till someone strong
pulls him back.

One summer in Rome I stood at Keats's
grave. Cats all over it, sprawling
on his nameless stone, the bench beside it,
the walk. I had to step over
the sacks of their bodies to get close
to his words: *Here lies one whose name
was writ in water.* And after visiting
the room of his death, I climbed
the Spanish steps half-way to view
his terrace from above. I took in

all of Keats that month, Hampstead,
the Nightingale's garden,
I even saw a brooch made from his hair.
What I most remember now
is how after Piazza di Spagna
I stopped for a glass of water

and then I couldn't drink it, I swear,
my throat closed
and it wouldn't go down.

Have you ever crossed a bridge at dusk
when the lights blaze on,
and there you are, lifted over formlessness
by a few strands of light?
Have you felt blessed, as if given
over to the gods or magic, saying *yes*
as if you had, all along, been praying for
just this? It's the emptiness, I suppose, the need
to pass through it, or over it,
to place one image in front of
the other, stepping across words

you didn't prepare yourself for saying.
Listen. I didn't know
I would mention the birch here,
how we woke the first day of November

to find the tree bending, the deck a sudden mass
of snow-covered veins and tongues, a tangle of gold
hair and white. My daughter
leaned into the curve of branches
and became the gesture
meant to restore them.
She gathered them in like aging women
a few at a time, pulling them close to her
body. Swiftly, she came up

to release them from heavy snow,
to toss them back
into the gaping
air. It took two days

for the tree to rise again. It took till now
for me to say it: it is the poem
that saves me. Do you hear? It is crossing the water
of *Sunday Morning* through a bird-filled sky,
or reaching across the Susquehanna,
its tight bridge like a throat
I didn't know could swallow or speak.

Suddenly, Fruit

Perhaps you have been told the wrong
story—how I was betrayed by the flower,
the earth's mouth opening to swallow
only me, the rape, the rape.
Maybe I was out there thumping
in tall grass, tired of the frivolity,
the dancing and pastels, wanting
complexity; something deeper, a taste
of where Death lived. Perhaps he heard
my soles pounding discontentedly
and he appeared, curiously watching. I could tell you
it was love at first sight, a fiery submergence,
all passion and glow. But on the edges of that crack
we sat and talked, two worlds brought together
while the seasons kept changing
and we dangled our feet
into an airy sea. When I finally went,
it was to continue our conversation near the fire.
The light had grown too cool to hold us.
Our loss of body heat began to affect
what we were saying. See, he and I are not
responsible for buds or ice. We were talking
near the fire. Death kept filing by.
We grew hungry. Do you know how it is, Reader,
when two people hunger and suddenly
fruit floods your hands
and the fire dancing? I can't be
delicate about this. There was a choice.
I could have gone home and suppered on bread,
some cheese, a little white wine. But I had been gone
a long time. I was drenched in the colors
of hell. This sounds simple: if you don't

bite into the peeled fruit, it will
rot. If you don't press your glistening
mouths together, passing flesh and seeds
between, what will become of you?
The skin of the pomegranate gave way
in my fingers, and its fruit turned them red.

Acknowledgements

Several poems in *Suddenly, Fruit* first appeared in other publications: *Baybury Review*: "What We See Simply As Light"; *Cimarron Review*: "Planting, Memorial Days'" "After Hysterics" and "In a Room at the Tate"; *Evansville Review*: "A Body in the Pond"; *the eleventh muse*: "Cooking" and "Persephone at Gethsemane"; *The Louisville Review*: "In Castle Rest"; The MacGuffin: "Missing" and "The Fig Tree"; *Many Mountains Moving*: "Pageants" and "The Front Row"; *Paintbrush*: "Behind My Tongue"; *The Nebraska Review*: "Form"; *Red Brick Review*: "Suddenly, Fruit"; *The Spoon River Poetry Review*: "Glass."

Special thanks to Patrick Lawler, Annie Lighthart, David Lloyd, Julie Olin-Ammentorp and Mary Stebbins for their friendship and unwavering support.

The cover art for this book is "Pomegranate Orb"
and is pastel on paper, © 2006 Sue Sneddon.
The text of the book is typeset in 10-point Minion.
The book was designed by Lesley Landis Designs
and printed by Central Plains Book Manufacturing.